Adventure camp

An adventure camp programme

1 **Have you been on an adventure camp? Write.**

_____

2 **Read. Would you like to go on this adventure camp?**

T0344052

Today is Monday. Welcome to the adventure camp!

First, go through the front gate and wait by the white tent on your left. Angie, the camp helper, is waiting there. She will show you where you can pitch your tents.

Pitch your tents – we've got more tent pegs if you need them. Then, lay out your sleeping bags. When your tents are up, meet me at the white tent. We're going on a walk around the campsite.

We have most of our meals in the dining tent. It's the big green tent in the middle of the campsite. You can see it easily. When we go hiking or fishing, we have a packed lunch. Sometimes, we have a campfire. We can cook potatoes and fish on the fire. It's good fun!

Adventure Camp!

Remember to bring these things:

tent sleeping bag pegs compass rucksack torch

Please send in information about yourself by 20th May.

See you there!

Tomorrow we're going hiking. Bring your compasses. I hope you can read them! The activity is in the forest near the campsite. We're hiking through the forest to a small lake. Then we're fishing in the lake. I hope you are good at fishing – we're catching our dinner!

On Wednesday morning we're going swimming. You can swim in the lake but you can't swim in the river. In the afternoon we're going sailing on the lake.

On Thursday you can pack your rucksacks and take down the tents. We're going on a walk near the campsite before you go home.

3 **Read the text again. Then circle.**

1 The adventure camp is for *one week* / *four days* / *one month*.

2 The camp helper is waiting at the *white* / *green* / *red* tent.

3 They eat *all* / *some* / *most* of the meals in the dining tent.

4 They can't *swim* / *sail* / *fish* in the river.

4 **Read the text again. Then order.**

go fishing ☐

pack the rucksacks ☐

meet Angie ☐

swimming in the lake ☐

lay out the sleeping bags ☐

5 **Read the text again. Then match.**

1 Angie is ...

2 The dining tent ...

3 Sometimes ...

4 You can't ...

5 Bring compasses ...

a they have a campfire.

b for the hiking activity.

c is in the centre of the campsite.

d the camp helper.

e swim in the river.

6 **Read the text again. Then complete the adventure camp programme.**

Adventure Camp!

Monday	
Tuesday	
Wednesday	
Thursday	

7 **Look at the pictures. Then write.**

1

2

3

4

_____

_____

_____

_____

5

6

7

8

_____

_____

_____

_____

8 **Read. Then match.**

1	pitch	**a**	a fire
2	keep out	**b**	a compass
3	lay out	**c**	a tent
4	light	**d**	the rain
5	put in	**e**	the bed
6	read	**f**	the pegs

9 **Read and write. Then find and circle.**

1 You use this at night to see.   t _ _ _ _ _

2 You put your clothes here when hiking.   r _ _ _ _ _ _ _

3 You use them to pitch a tent.   p _ _ _

4 You sit around this at night.   f _ _ _

5 A big area of water.   l _ _ _

6 A place with a lot of trees.   f _ _ _ _ _

7 This helps you read a map.   c _ _ _ _ _ _

8 You need a fishing rod to do this.   f _ _ _ _ _ _

R	A	V	U	K	F	J	A
U	P	Z	C	G	I	L	L
C	E	L	C	M	S	P	A
K	T	H	O	V	H	D	K
S	I	D	M	F	I	R	E
A	S	T	P	O	N	L	E
C	P	N	A	R	G	S	D
K	M	S	S	E	H	O	E
W	A	Q	S	S	G	E	P
H	C	R	O	T	S	R	Y

Remember!

Use at for times, on with days of the week and in for parts of the day (except with night).
We arrive at three o'clock.
We are going fishing on Saturday.
There are activities in the morning **and** in the afternoon.
We'll see the stars at night.

10 **Complete an adventure camp programme. Use your own ideas.**

Monday	
Tuesday	
Wednesday	
Thursday	

11 **Look at Activity 10 and answer these questions. Then write about a trip to an adventure camp.**

- Where is the camp?
- What can/can't you do?
- What do/don't you like doing?
- What do you need to take?

TIP!

A programme tells people what they can do, when and where.

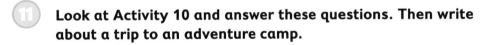

1   **Should animals be kept in zoos? What do you think? Write.**

2   **Now read. Do you agree?**

<u>Today, a lot of animals are kept in zoos.</u>
<u>Which is better for the animals: to live in zoos or in the wild?</u>

Some people think that animals should live in the wild and not in zoos because zoos are different to their natural environment. The weather is different. The food is different. The animals around them are different. There are more people around. Zoos are often small. Animals have to live in cages or walk up and down in a small area. And in zoos the animals don't need to look for food or protect themselves and they lose their natural instincts.

Other people think zoos are better and safer for wild animals. For example, some monkeys and birds are nearly extinct because people are destroying their homes. Other animals are nearly extinct because people hunt them for their fur – tigers for example. Zoos protect these animals and help them to survive.

I think animals should live in the wild. But we have to stop people hunting the animals for their fur and destroying their homes. If people don't stop hunting animals, then zoos are good because the zoos can help to protect the animals. I think we have to look after animals because they share our planet.

3 **Read the text again. Then complete.**

Wild animals should live in zoos because ...	Wild animals shouldn't live in zoos because ...
It's safer.	

4 **Read the text again. Then circle.**

1 Some people think that animals should live in the wild because ...
   a it's safer.
   b people are destroying their homes.
   c zoos are too small for them.

2 Some animals are nearly extinct because ...
   a they don't have any fur.
   b people are destroying their homes.
   c people protect their homes.

3 Zoos can help to ...
   a protect animals.
   b destroy animals' homes.
   c keep animals' natural instincts.

5 **Read the text again. Then match.**

1 An animal that doesn't exist any more.   **a** hunt
2 A small area where some animals live in a zoo.   **b** cage
3 To look for and kill an animal.   **c** zoo
4 A place where animals are kept.   **d** protect
5 Make sure animals are kept safe.   **e** fur
6 The hair of an animal.   **f** extinct

6 **Unscramble. Then match.**

1 relttu
_ _ _ _ _ _

a An animal with stripes that lives in the jungle.

A

2 ornhi
_ _ _ _ _

b A river animal.

B

3 lhewa
_ _ _ _ _

c This animal lives in water but lays eggs on the beach.

C

4 griet
_ _ _ _ _

d One of the fastest members of the cat family.

D

5 ecetahh
_ _ _ _ _ _ _

e The white one is almost extinct.

E

6 ttroe
_ _ _ _ _

f An animal that lives in the sea and is hunted.

F

7 **Read. Then write. Which are the ...?**

| biggest | ~~fastest~~ | heaviest | lightest | longest | slowest | tallest |

1 Cheetahs are some of the fastest animals.
2 Elephants are some of the _____ and _____ animals.
3 Giraffes are _____ .
4 Mice are some of the _____ .
5 Turtles _____ .
6 Snakes _____ .

8 **Find out. Then sort and write. Add more animals to the groups.**

| butterfly | dinosaur | elephant | frog | mouse | octopus |
| otter | panda | snake | spider | swan | turtle | worm |

Group A: _____

Group B: _____

Group C: _____

How have you grouped the animals?

_____

_____ .

Remember!

When writing your opinion:
- **Start with a** topic sentence.
- **Start a** new paragraph **to introduce each** different point of view.
- **End with a** personal opinion.

9   Look, think and plan. Then write.

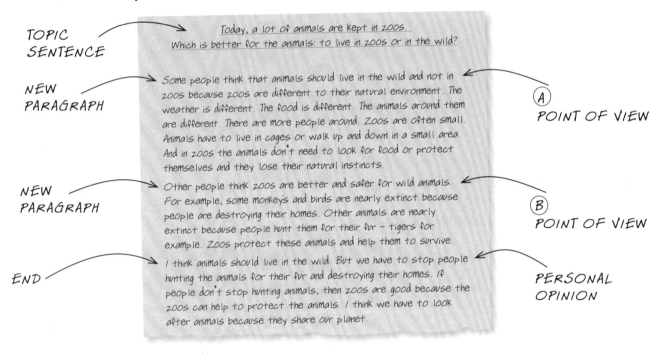

TOPIC SENTENCE

NEW PARAGRAPH

NEW PARAGRAPH

END

A POINT OF VIEW

B POINT OF VIEW

PERSONAL OPINION

Today, a lot of animals are kept in zoos. Which is better for the animals: to live in zoos or in the wild?

Some people think that animals should live in the wild and not in zoos because zoos are different to their natural environment. The weather is different. The food is different. The animals around them are different. There are more people around. Zoos are often small. Animals have to live in cages or walk up and down in a small area. And in zoos the animals don't need to look for food or protect themselves and they lose their natural instincts.

Other people think zoos are better and safer for wild animals. For example, some monkeys and birds are nearly extinct because people are destroying their homes. Other animals are nearly extinct because people hunt them for their fur – tigers for example. Zoos protect these animals and help them to survive.

I think animals should live in the wild. But we have to stop people hunting the animals for their fur and destroying their homes. If people don't stop hunting animals, then zoos are good because the zoos can help to protect the animals. I think we have to look after animals because they share our planet.

- Is it good for animals to be in cages? Why/Why not?
- Are there any zoos near you? Do you visit it/them?
- What can we do to protect animals?

1 What are some of the most interesting places in your city or village? Write.

2 Read this description. Is it similar or different to your village?

Richmond upon Thames is a town in the south east of England. It is about fifteen miles from the centre of London. It is a very pretty town. People have visited it for hundreds of years, including many famous people.

The River Thames goes through Richmond. Today many tourists travel up and down the river by boat. From the river you can see the famous palace of King Henry VIII, Hampton Court.

There is also a royal park in Richmond, called Richmond Park. Many years ago the Royal Family used to hunt deer in the park. Today no one hunts in the park but when you visit, you can still see the deer.

Getting there

It takes about twenty minutes to get to Richmond from London on the fast train. You can also get to Richmond from London on the underground. This is slower.

Where to stay

There are a lot of nice hotels and guest houses in Richmond. Some of the hotels are on Richmond Hill near the park. Others are next to the river.

Shopping

Richmond isn't a very big town but it's got all of the most popular shops. There are also lots of cafés in the town centre.

Things to do

In Richmond there are lots of things to do. There is a sports centre with an indoor and an outdoor swimming pool. There is also a stadium. If you like watching films or seeing a play, there are some cinemas and theatres.

Richmond upon Thames

Richmond upon Thames

3 **Read the text again. Then circle.**

1 Richmond is …

   a in the centre of London.

   b on a river.

   c in the south west of England.

2 The quickest way to get to Richmond from London is by …

   a tube.

   b train.

   c bicycle.

3 Richmond is …

   a on the River Thames.

   b in the River Thames.

   c at the River Thames.

4 Kings and queens used to … in Richmond Park.

   a run

   b relax

   c hunt

5 Hampton Court is a …

   a castle.

   b royal palace.

   c park.

4 **Read the text again. Then circle _True_ (T) or _False_ (F).**

1 Richmond has had many visitors for a long time.   T / F

2 Hampton Court Palace is on the River Thames.   T / F

3 There aren't any deer in Richmond Park today.   T / F

4 You can go swimming in the sports centre.   T / F

5 There aren't any cinemas in Richmond.   T / F

5 **Read the answers. Then write questions about Richmond.**

1 _____ ?

You can get to London by train.

2 _____ ?

Near the park and also next to the river.

3 _____ ?

From the river.

4 _____ ?

By boat.

6 **Look at the pictures. Then write.**

1

2

3

4

5

6

7

8

7 **Read. Then complete.**

bookshop   bus stop   railway station   sports centre   university

My big brother goes to ¹_____. Every day he catches the bus from the ²_____ outside our house and goes to the ³_____ where he catches the train to Edinburgh. After he's finished studying, he plays tennis. He belongs to a tennis club, which is next to the ⁴_____. When he's not playing tennis or studying, he's in the local ⁵_____ buying more books to add to the hundreds he's already got!

8 **What places can you find in a village, city and in both?**

airport   bookshop   bus stop   chemist   cinema   circus   college
factory   fire station   guest house   newsagent   post office   railway station
shopping centre   stadium   theatre   underground   university

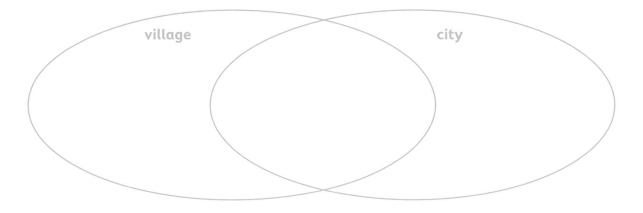

village   city

Remember!

When we write about a town, we write information under different headings.
Where to stay
Getting there

9   **Think about your village/city or a place you know well. Complete the mind map to make some notes and plan your writing. Then write about it.**

How to
get there

Where
is it

My town,
village, city

Where to
stay

Where to go
shopping

What to do

TIP!

Try to include practical and interesting information that will make people want to visit.

1 Has anything funny or strange happened to you? Write.

_____

2 Read. Has something similar happened to you?

_____

What a day! by Sonia   Blog

First, I woke up late. I usually hear the alarm clock but today I didn't. I didn't have time for breakfast and I missed my bus. I arrived at school fifteen minutes late. I forgot my lunch box. My friends gave me some of their lunch. Then we had P.E. It was Tuesday. Tuesdays are swimming days. I didn't have my swimsuit, so I spent the afternoon helping one of the teachers to tidy the P.E. cupboard. Great!

I left school at four o'clock and walked to the bus stop. There were police cars everywhere. 'Oh no! What's the problem now?' The road was closed.

We waited and waited and waited. An hour later, a bus came. We got on the bus. A group of ladies were angry because they had to wait. But we still didn't know what the problem was. It was seven o'clock when I got home. Mum was really worried. I was in big trouble. And I left my mobile phone at school!

I ate my dinner and heard the news. 'And here's the latest news on the two robbers who stole ten computers from Lakehurst School earlier this afternoon. The robbers were outside the school in a black van at 4 o'clock. All the roads around the school have been closed. The police think the robbers were dangerous. The school will be closed all week.'

What a day!

3 **Read the text again. Then match.**

1 Sonia forgot	a were closed.
2 Two robbers stole computers	b was worried.
3 The roads around the school	c from Lakehurst School.
4 Sonia's mum	d her lunch box.

4 **Read the text again. Then circle *True* (T) or *False* (F).**

1	Sonia had breakfast before going to school.	T / F
2	Sonia didn't want any lunch.	T / F
3	Sonia left her swimsuit at home.	T / F
4	The bus went back to the school.	T / F
5	Sonia heard some news about the robbers.	T / F
6	The robbers had a black van.	T / F

5 **Read the text again. Then circle.**

1 Sonia …
   a has an alarm clock to wake her up.
   b usually misses the bus.
   c usually forgets her lunch box.

2 On Tuesdays Sonia normally …
   a has P.E.
   b goes swimming.
   c helps tidy the P.E. cupboard.

3 The robbers …
   a were outside the school in a black van.
   b spoke to the people on the bus.
   c spoke to the driver.

4 Sonia was in trouble because …
   a her mum was worried.
   b she left her mobile phone at school.
   c she forgot her lunch box.

6 **Look at the pictures. Then write.**

1

_____

2

_____

3

_____

4

_____

5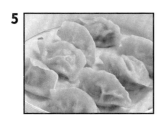

_____

6

_____

7

_____

8

_____

7 **Unscramble. Then match.**

1 emeteleot   _ _ _ _ _ _ _ _ _

2 istaephtg   _ _ _ _ _ _ _ _ _

3 alpael   _ _ _ _ _ _

4 ewts   _ _ _ _

5 ruryc   _ _ _ _ _

6 isuhs   _ _ _ _ _

a A combination of vegetables (beans, potatoes, etc.) and meat.

b Originally from India.

c Made from eggs.

d Made up with rice and fish.

e A long thin type of pasta.

f Spanish rice dish.

Match. Then make sentences.

1 miss

2 drop

3 pack

4 pass

a my school bag

b a test

c the bus

d a ball

1 _____ .

2 _____ .

3 _____ .

4 _____ .

Remember!

Use an exclamation mark (!) to add emphasis.
Oh no!
Wow!
That's great!
I'm hungry!

9 **Write ! or ?.**

1 I arrived at school fifteen minutes late ___

2 The bus driver drove back to school ___

3 Oh, no ___

4 What's the problem now ___

10 **Write your true story.**

- Where were you?
- What were you doing?
- Who was there?
- What happened?

TIP!

Use a lot of description in your story to make it sound even more exciting!

1. **What is the last book you read? Write.**

2. **Read. Would you like to read this book?**

Skellig

by David Almond

is the story of Michael.

Michael's family has moved to a house on the other side of town. Michael stays at his old school but now he has a long bus trip and he can't play football after school with his friends. He isn't happy in the new house. He is also unhappy because his baby sister is very ill.

The house is old. Outside there is a big garden and an old garage. Michael is not allowed to go into the garage. But one day, Michael goes into the garage. Inside he finds an old man called Skellig. Skellig lives in the garage. He eats flies and spiders. Skellig doesn't want anyone to know about him. It's Michael's secret. Michael takes food to Skellig and they become friends. One day Michael finds out that Skellig has wings. Michael wants to tell someone about Skellig. He decides to tell Mina, his new friend. Mina lives next door.

Mina is different to Michael's other friends. She doesn't go to school but she knows about everything. Mina's mother teaches her. She learns about nature and art and how to look and listen very carefully. Michael's friends think Mina is strange. Michael is happy when he is with Skellig and Mina.

This is a lovely story. It makes you feel happy and sad. You want to know about Mina, what happens to the baby, who Skellig is, if Michael's friends will be nice to him again. It's a book about everyday problems and it's a book that you will enjoy from beginning to end.

3 **Read the text again. Then circle.**

1 Michael is sad because ...
  a he has a new neighbour.
  b he hasn't got any friends near the new house.
  c he has a long bus trip.

2 The house ...
  a is new.
  b has a large garden.
  c is near his school.

3 Skellig ...
  a lives in the house next door.
  b eats insects.
  c wants everyone to know about him.

4 Mina ...
  a knows about Skellig.
  b has a teacher who comes to her house.
  c likes Michael's friends.

4 **Read the text again. Then match.**

a listens very carefully.	**1** Michael	**e** goes to school by bus.
b has got wings.	**2** Mina	**f** lives in a garage.
c loves nature.	**3** Skellig	**g** has got a baby sister.
d can't play football.		**h** doesn't go to school.

5 **Read the text again. Then number the sentences in order.**

Michael wants to tell someone about Skellig. ☐
Michael meets Skellig. ☐
Michael's family moves to a new house. ☐
Michael goes into the garage. ☐
Michael takes food to Skellig. ☐

6 **Look at the pictures. Then write.**

1

2

3

4

5

6

7

8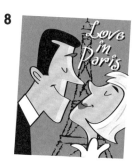

7 **Read. Then write.**

1 a story that is set in the future

2 a play which also has got songs in it

3 a scary story with action

4 a story told through pictures

5 a show or film that is funny

6 a love story

1		C		-			
2	M						
3				I			
4						N	
5					D		
6			A				

8 **Read. Then match.**

1 rock

2 blues

3 country

4 pop

5 jazz

a A style of music that has a complicated rhythm and often uses instruments like trumpets, saxophone, etc.

b Very commercial music.

c The most important instruments are the guitar and the drums.

d It originated in the USA but with the influence of African rhythms.

e Most cowboys and cowgirls like to dance to this music.

Remember!

We use because to give the reason why we think something.
I like this comedy because it is really funny.
I don't like this thriller because it isn't very interesting.

 Choose a book you've read or a film you've seen. Write about it.

- What was the title?
- What was the book/film about?
- What type of story was it?
- Who were the main characters? What were they like?
- How did the story develop?
- Why did/didn't you like it?

TIP!

A review helps people to decide if they want to read a book, see a film, etc., so if you don't like something, explain why!

1   **Where are you going on your next holiday? Write.**

_____

2   **Read. Would you like to visit Argentina?**

_____

Subject: A trip to Argentina

From: sue.spencer@homemail.com

This winter I am going on holiday to Argentina with my family. Argentina is in South America. It's a very big country and there's so much to see!

Argentina and Europe are on opposite sides of the equator. When it's winter here in Europe, it's summer in Argentina. That's why we are going in our winter holiday.

First we'll go to the Andes Mountains because my dad loves climbing. They're in a big national park in the west of the country.

Then we might visit one of the big farms in the middle of the country. My brother likes horses. On these farms, men ride horses to look after the cows.

Then we'll go to the beach. Mum loves beaches. There are lots of beaches in the east of the country on the Atlantic Ocean. I don't like beaches. I might ask dad to go to a water park or a boating lake when mum is on the beach!

Then we are going to the south. In summer you can go to the end of the country, which is nearly in Antarctica. Normally, you can't go there because it's too cold and there is a lot of ice and snow. But in summer it's possible to drive much further south.

Before we come back, we're going to Buenos Aires. That's the capital city of Argentina. We're going to watch some dancers dancing the *Tango*, a typical dance for two people. Argentina is famous for the tango.

And then we may go to an amusement park where we'll be able to go on a big wheel and a rollercoaster! I can't wait!

Sue

3 **Read the text again. Then circle.**

1 Argentina isn't in *South* / *North* America.

2 When it's summer in Europe, it's *summer* / *winter* in Argentina.

3 There are mountains in the *east* / *west* of the country.

4 In the centre of the country there are lots of *horses* / *farms*.

5 Sue's mum *is* / *isn't* going to go to a water park.

6 Sue's family is going to go to the south of Argentina by *plane* / *car*.

7 The tango is famous in *Spain* / *Argentina*.

4 **Read. Then match.**

1 the Andes	**a** Atlantic Ocean
2 farms	**b** capital city
3 tango	**c** mountain range
4 Buenos Aires	**d** rollercoaster
5 amusement park	**e** men on horseback
6 west	**f** dance

5 **Read the text again. Then complete.**

Andes   Antarctica   Atlantic   dance   farms   January   low   South America

1 Argentina is in _____ .

2 In _____ the weather is hot.

3 In July, the temperature is _____ .

4 Argentina is a big country. The _____ Mountains are in the west.

5 In the East is the _____ Ocean.

6 In the centre of the country there are a lot of big _____ .

7 The south is very cold in winter because it is near _____ .

8 Argentina is famous for its _____ .

6 **Read. Then match.**

1 A place where you can see fish and other sea creatures.

2 A place where kings and queens live.

3 A place where you can go on a rollercoaster.

4 A place where you can go sailing or swimming.

5 A place where you can see art or dinosaurs, for example.

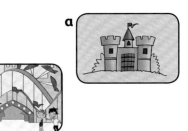

a

b

c

d

e

7 **Read. Then correct the mistakes.**

1 Last weekend I went to a park of amusement.

Last weekend I went to an amusement park.

2 First, we went on the wheel big.

3 Then we went on the lake of boats.

4 That was great. After that, we had a go on the golf mini.

5 Finally, we just had time to go on the dodge thems. I loved them!

8 **Read. Then find and circle.**

1 A place where you can see fish.
2 A place with towers built with stones.
3 A place where you can go on a water slide.
4 A ride that turns with colourful horses.
5 You go up and round in this.
6 A place where you can see old things.
7 A very big building with high walls.
8 Fun cars in an amusement park.

F	B	Y	U	S	L	P	U	O	C
W	A	T	E	R	P	A	R	K	A
A	Q	E	V	J	I	L	S	D	R
D	U	B	X	Q	O	A	H	O	O
C	A	S	T	L	E	C	K	D	U
C	R	N	L	P	D	E	Y	G	S
B	I	G	W	H	E	E	L	E	E
Z	U	L	E	N	W	Q	D	M	L
I	M	U	S	E	U	M	F	S	C

We use in the **when we talk about the directions:**
North, South, East **and** West.
in the east   in the west   in the north   in the south

9 **Imagine you are going on a trip soon. Write about it.**

- Where are you going?
- Who are you going with?
- What is the place like?
- What are you going to do there?

Subject:

From:

1 Have you ever been to a planetarium? If so, what was it like? If not, what do you think it's like? Write.

2 Read. Do you want to go?

A visit to the planetarium
by Anne, Class 5P

🪐 The plan

Last Thursday my class went to the planetarium in our town. Our town isn't very big and the planetarium is in the town centre. Mr Brown, our teacher, decided we could walk there. He loves walking! We took a letter home for our parents: 'Your child should wear warm clothes and a good pair of walking shoes. And he/she'd better take an umbrella because it might rain.'

🪐 Going to the planetarium

We left school at nine o'clock. It took twenty minutes to walk to the planetarium. It rained. Some children in my class had umbrellas but some others didn't. I had to share my umbrella with two of my classmates.

🪐 At the planetarium

When we got to the planetarium, we were cold and wet. We put our coats and umbrellas outside the room. Then a tall man showed the class where to go. It was frightening at first because it was very dark and I couldn't see anything. Then the show started. Wow! There were stars, planets and comets. It was amazing! We were in space! We saw Saturn and Mars and Venus and Neptune! It was incredible! After the show, we went to a classroom. In the classroom there were models of the Earth and planets. There were also lots of telescopes. Some were very old. They looked very complicated.

🪐 What I thought

The visit was fantastic! I didn't see everything, so I need to go again. Next time I think my parents should go too. It's one of the most amazing experiences I've ever had!

3 **Read the text again. Then match.**

1 The first paragraph is about ...   **a** what the children did at the planetarium.
2 The second paragraph is about ...   **b** Anne's opinion of the visit.
3 The third paragraph is about ...   **c** the preparations for the visit.
4 The last paragraph is about ...   **d** the journey to the planetarium.

4 **Read the text again. Then number the sentences.**

It was nine o'clock.

A man showed the class where to go.

Some children got wet.

The class took a letter home to their parents.

The class went into the telescope room.

5 **Order to make questions. Then read the text again and answer.**

1 did / the children / to / how / get / the planetarium

_____ ?

_____ .

2 all / have / did / the children / umbrellas

_____ ?

_____ .

3 Anne / did / which / planets / see

_____ ?

_____ .

4 the visit / enjoy / did / Anne

_____ ?

_____ .

6 **Read the answers. Then write questions about the text.**

1 _____ ?
On Thursday.

2 _____ ?
Mr Brown.

3 _____ ?
At nine o'clock.

4 _____ ?
She shared it with two classmates.

7 **Look at the pictures. Then write.**

8 **Read. Then complete.**

amazing	complicated	expensive	frightening
horrible	important	intelligent	interesting

We went to a really ¹ _____ place yesterday. I learned so much. We saw
models of ² _____ people, like kings and queens and presidents. It was
quite ³ _____ though. I think it was about £10 each! The teacher gave us
a worksheet to do. It was so ⁴ _____ I couldn't answer some of the
questions. Well, the really ⁵ _____ children answered all the questions!
Then we went into a castle. It was very dark and there were lots of strange noises.
It was quite ⁶ _____ . And the smell was ⁷ _____ ! We
got home in time for tea. What an ⁸ _____ day!

9 **Write (✔) or (✗). Then write correctly.**

1 afraid ☐ _____
2 carefull ☐ _____
3 noutghy ☐ _____
4 exiting ☐ _____
5 diferrent ☐ _____
6 difficult ☐ _____

Remember!

A heading describes the topic of a paragraph. It starts with a capital letter.
Where we went
What we saw

 Think of a visit to an interesting place. Then plan and write.

- What are you going to write about? (a visit to a planetarium? A visit to a theatre? A visit to a university?)
- What are you going to write first, second, etc.?
- What did you think about your visit?

Plan

A questionnaire

1 **Do you think people should reuse and recycle things? Why / Why not? Write.**

2 **Is Matthew environmentally friendly? And you? Read and write (✔) or (✗). Then check.**

	Questions	Points	
		Matthew	Me
1	Do you think it's important to recycle as many things as possible? (Think about paper, plastic cups, etc.)	✔	
2	Do you always recycle paper? (Think about using both sides of a sheet of paper, cutting the paper to the size you need, etc.)	✗	
3	Do you help to recycle plastic at home? (Think about plastic cups, plastic milk bottles, etc.)	✗	
4	Do you always turn off the lights when you leave a room? (Think about your bedroom, your classroom when you are last out, etc.)	✔	
5	Do you help to recycle bottles every week? (Think about sorting and recycling them by colour.)	✔	
6	When you go shopping with your parents, do you reuse plastic bags? (Think about taking an extra plastic bag with you.)	✔	
7	At school, do you help to collect rubbish in the playground? (Think about starting a club.)	✗	
8	Do you go to school by public transport or on foot? (Think about buses, trains, trams, underground, etc.)	✔	
9	Do you always try to keep your school clean? (Think about helping to clean the playground.)	✗	
10	Do you only buy new things, if you can't reuse them? (Think about clothes, books, mobiles, etc.)	✗	

8–10 points	5–7 points	Less than 5 points
Well done! You are really helping the environment. You try to recycle as many things as possible. Try and get more people to help you with your great work!	Not bad at all. You are already doing a lot to help the planet. Now try and do more. Ask your friends to help you and make it fun. You will soon be an environmental superstar!	It's great that you are doing something. What about doing more? Do one job for the environment every day. What you do is very important!

3   **Read the questionnaire again. Then write the number.**

1   Which question is about recycling clothes?   ☐

2   Which question is about recycling plastic bags?   ☐

3   Which question is about transports?   ☐

4   Which question is about lights?   ☐

5   Which question is about saving trees?   ☐

4   **Read the questionnaire again. Then match and write sentences.**

1 collect rubbish		**a** yoghurt pots, supermarket packaging
2 recycle plastic		**b** turn off lights in bedroom and classroom
3 only buy if can't reuse		**c** in the playground, starting a club
4 save energy		**d** mobile phones, books, clothes

1 _____ .

2 _____ .

3 _____ .

4 _____ .

5   **Look at Matthew's answers again. Then circle *True* (T) or *False* (F).**

1   Matthew doesn't think it's important to recycle.   T / F

2   Matthew always turns off the lights when he leaves a room.   T / F

3   Matthew reuses plastic bags when he goes shopping.   T / F

4   Matthew never goes to school by public transport.   T / F

5   Matthew only buys new things if he can reuse them.   T / F

6   Matthew always tries to keep his school clean.   T / F

6 **Look at the pictures. Then write.**

1  _____

2  _____

3  _____

4  _____

5  _____

6  _____

7  _____

8  _____

7 **Read. Then match.**

1 recycle paper   **a** reduce waste
2 recycle bottles   **b** conserve energy
3 collect rubbish   **c** save trees
4 reuse plastic bags   **d** keep the planet clean
5 turn off the lights   **e** reduce pollution
6 use public transport   **f** save resources

8 **Read. Then complete.**

| ambulance | clean | cut | fell down | ill | medicine |

I was helping to ¹_____ the house when I slipped on some water, ²_____ on the floor and ³_____ my knee! I didn't think much about it but later that evening, my knee hurt a lot and was very red. My mum called the doctor and he said to call an ⁴_____ . So there I was, at eleven o'clock, sitting in the waiting room at the hospital! There were a lot of very ⁵_____ people there. After three hours, I saw a doctor. He was very nice and said that I had to keep my leg up until my knee felt better and to take some ⁶_____ twice a day. So now I've got a great excuse for not doing the cleaning! But I'd prefer to clean than have a bad knee!

8   A questionnaire

Remember!

Yes/No questions **start with an** auxiliary verb.
Do **you recycle your clothes? No, I don't. / Yes, I do.**
Are **your parents going to use public transport? Yes, they are. / No, they aren't.**

9   **Read. Then correct.**

1   You do turn off the lights when leave you a room?

_____ .

2   You are a friend of the environment?

_____ .

3   You use public transport?

_____ .

4   You conserve energy?

_____ .

10   **Are your family and friends looking after the planet? Write a questionnaire.
Then ask them.**

1	What do you do to look after the planet?
2	How often do you recycle?
3	When do you recycle?
4	
5	
6	
7	
8	
9	
10	

A questionnaire is used to find out about people's opinions or habits and it shows us the different ideas that groups of people have about things.